Remotely Rich

Remotely Rich
Make $450K a Year as a Web Developer

by Matt Vogel

Remotely Rich

REMOTELY RICH
MAKE $450K A YEAR AS A WEB DEVELOPER

© 2016 Matt Vogel
Self-published
Portland, Oregon

All rights reserved.
No portion of this book may be reproduced in any form without the written permission of the publisher.

ISBN-13: 978-1534983052
ISBN-10: 1534983058

Printed in the United States of America.

Back cover photo credit: Hanna Blazer

Remotely Rich

Don't fear the reaper.
—Matt Vogel

Remotely Rich

Author's Note

This book was written based on my experience as an employed and remote developer. I assume no responsibility for any damages or legal issues resulting from the use of this book's content. This book should not be considered expert business, legal, marketing, accounting, tax or healthcare advice. I do not recommend or endorse unethical, illegal or deceptive practices in the application of ideas presented in this book.

Remotely Rich

PREFACE

Toughen up. I don't mean to get in your face right away, but I really do mean it. You've got to be confident and resilient to be a high-income, remote developer.

When I say you must be confident, I mean how you work with clients. From my experience, clients tend to walk all over you as a contractor… if you let them. You're the outsider, the line-item expense and the easiest person to blame for project delays and cost overruns. Too often, they're ready to make you the victim.

I'll cover more specifics about work issues throughout this book. But suffice it to say that you must communicate with clients from a position of strength in as professional a manner as you can under the circumstances.

This may involve telling clients what they don't want to hear or questioning their beliefs and assumptions about projects—even questioning their knowledge about programming and project management. There likely will be times when clients doubt your skills and value to projects, so you'll have to defend yourself.

Larger clients have tended to be easier for me to work with on many levels. Conflicts get resolved quickly because they have so many projects going on at once. Issues that demand my most confident attitude usually occur with mid-size and smaller clients. They feel more pressure to save money and intentionally or unintentionally look for ways to discount my work and time spent. This is when I need to speak up and make them respect what I bring to the work.

Okay, then there's resiliency. Fact: Some projects will be extremely frustrating to endure, for any number of reasons. So you've got to be resilient. This comes from being confident in your skills and in your toughness to stick with challenging projects to completion. Don't be a quitter unless an extraordinary circumstance arises that demands walking away. The fact is if you quit too easily you'll simply never make the big bucks.

Learn from awful projects or clients. Deposit the checks. Get over it and move on.

I guess that I think of contracts as sprints. You'll run fast and hard. Then it's over. If there's a headwind or rain in your face, suck it up and keep running hard. You must be in this game to win. That's the attitude I have… and it works.

Certainly this is very different than being in the position of a W-2 employee. Speak up too honestly or critically to managers and you'll probably lose your job. As a 1099 remote contractor, it's most likely that your clients need you more than you need them. They must respect you and the skills that you bring to their projects.

I apologize if it sounds like I've got a lot of attitude. Maybe I do. But it's based on sort of a survival instinct. My only goals are to do quality work, make my clients happy with the end products and make a boatload of money. To survive doing this, I have to be confident and resilient. For you to win at this game like I have, you must do the same thing.

Remotely Rich

CONTENTS

Introduction 1

My Story 5

Making the Big Bucks 13

Landing the Contracts to Grow Your Business 23

Got the Contract… Now What? Onboarding 35

Golden Rules 43

The 1099 Versus W-2 Mentality 51

Setting Up Your Business and Protecting Yourself 55

Working Remotely 65

Managing Client Expectations 71

Hiring Help 81

Self-care 87

Final Thoughts 93

Remotely Rich

Introduction

Let me come right out of the gate and ask you THE question. Do you want to make $450,000 a year as a Web developer? I've done it and can teach you how to do it too.

It's not rocket science. You don't need any special background or even an advanced education. Honestly, you don't even need to be the best of the best as a developer.

What you do need is a simple, practical strategy to leverage your current or future programming skills into a successful remote contracting business. Yes, this means you must want to be self-employed, because that's what blows the lid off employee salary ceilings. You also must have a pretty good understanding about where the money is today in the Web development industry—what customers want in Web site functionality and types of development tools to be used. And it also helps to be a bit ahead of the curve with trends in the marketplace and tools so you're prepared for inevitable change.

Of course you've got to have the skills that are in demand now. That means you should be a fairly accomplished developer or well on your way to that level. You need core skills beyond just one programming solution. Over-specialization can be risky and limit your market. A broad skill set with popular development tools opens the door to a vast number of customers and contracts. Simply put, versatility and decent competence with development tools means you can get jobs and deliver on what you apply for.

I can't emphasize enough that it takes a lot of work to generate an income approaching $450,000 a year. It takes sacrifice, focus, solid skills, grit, the confidence to deliver quality work and a certain amount of marketing of your skills to reach that income. Succeed at this and you'll build an ever-growing portfolio of happy clients and a skill set that will serve you well.

The rush of earning really good money is hard to describe. It's incredible to know that you're able to actually save a big chunk money each month after covering all the bills. And it's very rewarding to do this on your own terms, answering only to your customers and yourself.

After I give you a little background on my story to offer some perspective, I'll step you through everything you need to know to build a highly profitable remote developer business that you control. I won't be discussing how to code because you've got to start with that foundation or are in the process of getting those skills.

The chapters ahead will detail topics such as what's involved in making the big bucks, following the golden rules of workflow, understanding the mentality of an employee versus a vendor, establishing and operating your business, grasping the essentials about working remotely, managing client expectations, hiring help, finding leads and growing your business, taking care of yourself and work environment while working very hard, and rewarding yourself to enjoy the fruits of your labor.

If you've worked in-house as a developer or heard anything about what goes on behind the scenes, you know that experience is a good teacher and a source of interesting stories. I'll briefly highlight some of my experiences, not just for the entertainment value—although a few might make you wonder what the hell is going on in our industry—but mainly for the lessons learned.

So let's get you started on a path to more control over your life and earning some serious money.

Remotely Rich

Chapter 1
My Story

Just so you know, I have no special advantages or background that launched me quickly to success as a Web developer.

My dad is a garbage truck driver and my mother sold garbage removal services. I only have a high school education. The truth is that I wasn't even going to graduate. Unfortunately, I skipped too many classes and got expelled. So I transferred to a lower credit requirement high school. Eventually I was a little lucky to graduate from an alternative program with the "troubled" kids and pregnant teen moms. So as far as education is concerned, it's not like I was a star student on a path to an Ivy League school.

My journey to becoming a successful developer started when I got a lucky break and landed a job in a computer store. It was just a sales job—maybe for a year—but I did become familiar with the latest hardware and software. I don't think I consciously recognized industry trends or anything. Or maybe the thing I did register in the back of my mind was that I was interested in working in the computer or technology industry. I'd always been fascinated by technology and even got into building computers while working at the store. The potential of computers and the Web were obvious to me.

My next job was at AT&T. I was hired to manually (by hand) change addresses in their billing system. My curiosity in programming led me to find a way to partially automate my job by writing macros in the mainframe terminal. This saved me time and effort. It also got me noticed by my managers.

After a short time, I got promoted. Another department figured that they could use someone with my macro writing experience. So already I was learning how to build depth in a marketable skill to move up the ranks. Eventually, I was promoted to an analyst position. That's when I learned how to use Visual Basic to control software tools. I loved being able to create the functions and make the tools more useful.

This is the time when I also became more uncomfortable working within a large company in an office environment. Everyone in the department was at least 20 years older than I. They were torn between respecting me for my growing skills and resenting me for having the same title as they had but at only the age of 19. Without getting into the details, let's just say that there was plenty of friction. I knew my days there probably were numbered.

So my stint at AT&T set the tone for my move to self-employment. To be perfectly frank, I learned that I didn't like working in a company office at all. It felt a lot like being a slave or not being treated like an adult. There's always someone watching you. Someone else determines the time you work, when you eat lunch, the projects you work on, the people you work around and how much you can earn.

Another challenge about working for a company in an office was use of the popular software development methodology, Agile. It's about self-organizing, cross-functional teams with adaptive planning, an evolutionary development process and continuous improvement. That sounded great. But for the developers doing the work, it meant always checking in and explaining what you were doing that day and the day before. And this usually took place in open offices close to a bunch of other people. Honestly, you even lost your cubicle—the one bit of privacy you could have in an office.

Let's just say that all of this wasn't a good fit for my personality and professional goals. This office environment just wasn't something I could picture myself enduring for long. That said, I must admit that it was a slow evolution to transition from having a job to thinking seriously about contracting.

The saving grace for all this was that I discovered from various managers that developer work could be done remotely. I'd heard about developers doing it successfully but it almost sounded like another urban legend. Would companies really hire developers outside their sphere of control? Did they have all that much work that couldn't be covered by in-house employees? Well, the managers I talked with said yes to these questions. And they even said that the money could be really good if I managed my workload properly and got the right jobs.

Originally, I just put my résumé online on a job site and employers found me. Calls poured in. It might have looked like I was padding my résumé a bit back then to generate so much interest. But hey, a big factor in that interest was the amount of demand in the market for almost any level of Web developer.

The truth was that my résumé just listed lots of important key words about elements of projects I had worked on. I may not have had that much of a track record with certain functions of development tools or many projects in a variety of areas. But, I did have at least some work experience associated with them. The key was that I knew I could deliver on projects requiring certain skills for everything I included in my résumé.

Project after project, my credentials kept growing. The more I learned on-the-job, the more I could build my résumé for the next job. Every single job had higher requirements, and thus, paid more money. The upward curve in jobs I got and the resultant income was amazing.

I often say that I "quit my way" to the top. In other words, I got better and better contracts by leaving at some point or arranging it so my contract wasn't extended—all to move on and up. This practice was all about knowing the cloud of skills to cultivate to keep advancing my hourly rate and meeting higher project requirements. These were the clues that pointed toward a winning strategy to earn a very high income.

Once I got rolling as a self-employed Web developer, the job acquisition process got way easier. Staffing agency recruiters called all the time due to the demand for remote services that their clients couldn't handle or that they just outsourced. I also found projects posted every day, mainly through staffing agencies but occasionally directly from potential customers.

Of course, I didn't get every job I applied for. And don't get me started on the topic of overseas outsourcing and how it affects competition for work. Anyway, I never have a problem getting work for my target types of projects to maintain a mid-six figure income.

My story is all about being willing to work very hard. That means long days, many evenings and weekends. You have to be ready to go all-in. Do it like I did and you'll win.

The experience of success at this level was truly transformational. I got out of debt and moved out on my own. I saved money faster than I ever dreamed I could. Even my perspective on money changed. Instead of thinking in terms of hundreds or even thousands of dollars of income, I started thinking about tens of thousands and hundreds of thousands of dollars. What I always thought were big expenses, quickly seemed trivial.

Importantly, I could invest in myself with no hesitation. I also could think about work tasks that I could delegate. In a way, my work was legitimized as I established my office and contracted for support services that I didn't want to do myself.

Yes, success in a monetary sense is very liberating. But I can't think of anything more thrilling than helping you experience this same payoff for doing great work as a developer. It's the payoff you deserve.

On the subject of payoffs, I feel compelled to mention a funny aspect related to my early success. It regards the reactions I got from family and friends. As I began earning in the five figures per month, people close to me seemed to be happy for me but also were in disbelief. They really couldn't wrap their heads around this non-college educated guy making so much money

They spoke about what I was doing as if it were temporary or that "the other shoe was going to drop" at some point so my work would evaporate. Surely I couldn't continue this indefinitely, in their minds. Part of this was that they wanted to protect me from the horizon of dashed hopes. I just laughed and kept going. Most of my family and friends finally did recognize the business I created and its staying power. Maybe all of the stories about successful young startup founders have made experiences like mine more believable.

Before we start talking specifically about making the big bucks as a programmer, I should mention a very important lesson I learned from my mother about customer service. It's at the core of my story.

The only way you'll be able to achieve success using my business strategy is to provide outstanding service to your clients.

My mom always has been a successful outside salesperson. She has had a way of delivering superior customer service that builds trust, confidence and creates lasting relationships. She taught me by example to be attentive to clients through my communications with them and even when I'm not communicating with them.

When communicating with clients, Mom taught me that the most important habit to have is to be clear, authentic, detailed and confident with them. When not communicating, she stressed the value of imagining what clients might be thinking about with regard to the project and my services. She would develop a picture of their concerns or try to read where their heads were at any given moment. Her goal was to remain in their good graces and stay a step ahead in the game serving their needs. This way she could anticipate when needs weren't being met, when extra communication was a good idea and when concerns might arise.

I've found this to be a critical strategy as I operate at a high workload level. To keep the plates spinning—keeping on track with projects and client relationships—I must be proactive. It's just too late if all I do is react to issues, changes and surprises. Please keep this in mind as you read the next chapter.

Remotely Rich

Chapter 2
Making the Big Bucks

What's the secret type of work that's going to get you to the $450,000 per year level? Actually, the type of work isn't a secret at all. It's contract developer jobs with a range of pay levels, various durations and a variety of skills required. These are contracts announced directly by companies, through staffing agencies and advertised via online job platforms.

To earn the big bucks you will be working three full-time jobs simultaneously. Yes, this sounds crazy but let me explain.

Let me be more specific about the pay. I'd say that earning $10,000 to $12,000 per month for <u>each</u> job is very realistic. This means you'll typically average around $70 per hour for each job. That translates into about $30,000 per month total for the projects when you strategically select your three jobs to handle simultaneously.

Okay, about the full-time work. The fact is that even when these contracts are presented by employers as "full-time" remote jobs, they actually are not full-time. The 40-hour workweek is a myth, at least in the programming arena. Nearly all contracts require only about 20 hours of work each week to complete the expected tasks. This is how you can manage three supposedly full-time contracts at the same time as a self-employed Web developer.

Think of it this way. Clients use the frame of reference of in-house W-2 employees. When you subtract unnecessary meetings, distracting calls and emails, irrelevant co-worker conversations, and other non-programming activities typical in workplaces, you're left with far fewer than 40 hours per week spent actually programming.

I propose that you do what I do by leveraging this situation to your advantage. Clients get the results and value they expect, so they're happy. You skip all of the wasted distractions from actual work, so you can focus on the work you want. Your reward for being so efficient is the payment you deserve.

Basically, I consider contracting similar to being on retainer. Managers have project budgets and timelines that serve as the basis for contract work—it's all that really counts to them. In the scheme of things, they've budgeted for tasks to be completed not really the hours even though that's the traditional measure.

To summarize, companies that hire Web developers are results-based. Your hourly pay for time not spent on their projects basically is your reward for working very efficiently and maintaining a high quality of work. It's not much different than working for flat rates per project, where your bonus is being able to come in under budget. So there's nothing unethical or un-business-like to this.

It's critical to remember that you must be looking to work full-time to make the big bucks. I probably average working 10-14 hours a day, often seven days a week. Sometimes weekends are lighter so I have time to take care of personal activities and enjoy a little social life. But the goal is to maximize earnings and make sure that all deliverables to clients are kept on schedule.

Contract remote job titles and descriptions provided by employers and staffing agencies vary in quality and accuracy. The first two key words you must look for are "developer" and "remote." Most of the time, the descriptions include the programming languages required or desired for the projects, which is key to making sure the project is in your wheelhouse of skills.

To strategically select the right jobs, you really need to focus on your existing skills. Ideal jobs are ones that you're qualified to handle very efficiently. In other words, you have the appropriate tools (software and computer), skills in programming languages and experience—or at least very close to this—for each job. There usually are indicators in the language of job descriptions that can serve as good signs or red flags.

There are quite a few annual surveys of advertised programming jobs that identify the most in-demand languages. For example, they list SQL, Java, Javascript, C#, Python, C++, PHP, IOS, Ruby on Rails, etc. Aside from checking these details in job descriptions, it's good to keep up on what's popular so you have the appropriate skills for the greatest number of jobs. If you're over-specialized or don't have in-demand skills, it's going to be far more challenging to find an adequate number of jobs to keep your revenue high.

One thing that I've never quite figured out is the value of becoming a sort of evangelist for a particular programming language. Some developers preach that a single language is the answer to all programming needs. While some languages certainly are versatile, this philosophy really locks you in and limits your marketability to those who don't agree with you.

I wouldn't want to spend my valuable time trying to convince clients that my one specialty is the answer to their every need. I'd rather be the utility player who has solid skills in the most popular languages and can work in their comfort zone. So again, success results from riding the wave of demand with the right strategy.

Back to job descriptions, I can't emphasize enough that you're looking for descriptions that clearly state what the employer wants you to do. Good job descriptions are very factual and present a straightforward hiring process. Boilerplate type job descriptions often can be a good sign, as long as they're specific enough that the job is accurately presented. Too general a description could mean that they're playing games with their hiring. This often ends up with you spending too much time in the interview process and/or competing with other developers—maybe for a job that doesn't even make sense for you after the true details are revealed.

You want to avoid descriptions that indicate lots meetings and hints about their desire to "indoctrinate" you into their culture to align your work with their mission. For example they might say, "looking for epic coder, but tell us about you rather than send résumé" or maybe they'll ask for your Twitter account or other personal submissions. And be alert for any hints about extra time requirements such as excessive reporting to multiple team members or training they want you to have in areas not directly relevant to the project.

All of this might be different if you're heading for an in-house, full-time position, but none of this works for contractors who are hired just to get the work done. Your mantra is efficiency.

Below is what I consider to be a perfect job description for a remote developer.

Python Django Developer
Rate: $75/hour, W2/1099/c2c
Location: 100% Remote
Interview Type: Telephone/Skype

Required Skills:
Latest Django (1.7/1.8)
Django rest framework
Python 2.7/3
Neo4J or graph DB knowledge
Mysql schema best practices
Social API integration experience
Django CMS
Strong experience in multitasking and coordinating multiple ongoing projects.

> Nice to haves: (NOT REQUIRED)
> Gitflow best practices
> Ability to work off of, and make educated decisions based on, evolving requirements
> Oauth2 experience
> Writing Django tests
> AngularJS
> SOLR
> Vagrant
> Haystack
> Python Twisted experience
> ETL experience
> Queuing experience
> Pep8 compliance

Why is this a perfect job description? For starters, the rate is clearly stated and it's competitive. Then, there is a corporation-to-corporation option that lets you take advantage of tax breaks. It's clearly noted that this position will be 100% remote, not "a few days a week" or "must come into the office every other week" or anything like that.

It's clearly stated what the "must haves" are for this position—skills that are required. It includes a "nice to haves" section. This is very helpful, so you can speak to as many of these items as you can to score extra points and tip the hiring decision in your favor.

Notice that there is no emotional language used. There aren't statements such as "excited about our mission," "wants to learn more," or "self starter." These are unnecessary and do not serve to filter potential candidates.

Also, the interview can be conducted remotely. Some remote positions still want you to fly there to meet face-to-face, which definitely can interfere with your other projects.

Certainly not all job descriptions will match this example. You'll see quite a range out there. But this one should give you a target to look for.

So just to be sure you understand, the jobs you're looking for are temporary employee or contract (IRS 1099), not in-house employment (IRS W-2). Job descriptions that require on-site work should be a deal breaker, because you won't be able to perform your other contract work there. You're looking to remain off-site and self-employed, for the control over how you spend your time, earnings potential and business tax breaks.

Small companies may have way more project oversight and day-to-day involvement with you, so they might be more hour-conscious. These are not the companies you want to work with for this and other reasons, unless you have a very compelling reason to do so. Larger companies or organizations have the scale of projects, resources, budgets and processes that are far more compatible with high-revenue contracting like I do and you should do.

Of course, there's nothing wrong with taking on jobs that have different time requirements. For example, you might line up two fairly large contracts and maybe one smaller one. The key is to look for contracts that reflect the workload you want to establish for a given period. If you want a bit more free time one month, then you should look for a couple of smaller contracts. Also, if your workload is light and you want to kick it up for a while, you might take on a couple of extra smaller contracts. That said, be careful not to get stuck with a small contract or two that hinders your ability to line up larger contracts. Veering from three substantial simultaneous contracts likely will result in lower earnings.

Ideal contracts are for projects that take months to complete and offer a strong potential for contract extensions. These are stable revenue generators and allow you to reduce the time you spend interviewing for and onboarding with new clients. You want to establish yourself as a valued long-term asset. This is so managers will find projects for you even after your initial one is finished just to keep the contract relationship intact.

In a more technical sense, ideal clients provide very clear instructions, great quality code and a build using tools you are very familiar with. They also have the time and money to do the job right. How often does this happen? I'm sorry to say not very frequently. The reality is more like a scale that ranges from bad to great, with most clients and projects rating somewhere around the middle.

By maintaining their contracts with you, it makes their lives easier too. It means they don't need to go through the hiring process again with all of the associated delays. The work gaps in these cases typically are short. It's what I call being in a "holding pattern" doing minor jobs—sometimes things like writing some documentation or other activities connected with programming—or nothing while still on the employer's contract payroll. Always say yes to these offers, unless you honestly cannot do the work. As I said, maintaining an active status with employers saves you job shopping time and keeps the revenue flowing.

To wrap up this topic, I recommend that you get over the natural feeling that you cannot have three full-time jobs at once. Also, I urge you to become a discerning contract job shopper. You're looking for good signs that the jobs are exactly what you want and avoid spending any time on jobs with too many red flags. Efficiency, efficiency, efficiency. That's the name of the game to earn the big bucks.

Okay, one story about job descriptions since I ranted about those being so pivotal. I've learned not take job descriptions too seriously. Often, they can be as deceptive as they seem to be straightforward.

I once applied for a job that stressed the importance of the candidate being a "technical leader." Sounds good, right? Then again, this could be that they were just trying to make the job sound important.

It turned out that three company developers conducted my interview. I gathered I had to pitch that I'm a leader in some way plus know my stuff on the skills side. Everything seemed to move along well until they called me a "polyglot developer." That could be a compliment in some cases, but not this time. Basically, I oversold myself. They said they were worried that the project would be too boring for me.

This was a legit job, but it also was a sort of bait and switch with the misleading emphasis on being a leader. In other words, the description didn't match the reality of the work. It was a big waste of my time.

Unfortunately, this misleading recruitment process happens too often. I think it's a conscious effort by companies to ensure that they attract overqualified candidates so they can talk them into lower pay rates. So the lesson learned is to be a bit skeptical about the language used in job descriptions.

Chapter 3
Landing the Contracts to Grow Your Business

Before I get into the process of landing the right contracts, I want to mention a couple thoughts about working with staffing agencies. Most of your developer contracts will come through agencies. The main reason is that they save employers considerable time pre-screening and interviewing candidates.

Occasionally, employers will solicit contractors directly for certain types of projects or if the employer is pretty small and wants to avoid agencies' placement fees. But I'd say that the vast majority of developer contracts are advertised and solicited by agencies.

The more agencies you can work through at any given time, the more options you'll have for contracts. You want to maximize your opportunities to get contracts and not all agencies will place developers with the full range of employers out there. Many agencies have their own relationships with particular employers—sometimes exclusives—or they might specialize in certain industries.

Agencies will ask you to sign a "right to represent" agreement. I recommend that you sign those, as they're required for your résumé to be submitted to clients. This just states that the staffing agency is the only one representing you for a particular contract. This does not prevent you from working with other agencies to apply for other contracts.

Another thing about working with agencies is that you can end up wasting a lot of time filling out online forms for them. Occasionally they want you to enter all types of personal information and details that are more for their purposes than for any employer. And some agencies want you to complete the same big set of forms every time a contract comes along that fits your skills. That's ridiculous and costly for you due to the application/interview time involved.

Your résumé and maybe some coding samples are all most employers are looking for. I'll complete the forms necessary for the specific contract so the employer has what it needs. If the agency rep wants to enter the other data, fine.

Whether an agency submits your résumé to an employer or you send it directly, make sure it focuses on your skills and relevant types of projects you've handled. Load it with keywords, such as the names of programming languages, frameworks, libraries and packages you know and words that describe methodologies from your development work. And, importantly, the more your résumé can be customized for each job the better. You want to concentrate on what specific employers care about, which are their unique projects, business area, audience or customers, and potentially other aspects that they disclose.

What about samples of your work? Being able to submit good coding samples can be crucial in landing jobs. Ideally, these are samples of work you've done for clients rather than from your personal projects. Non-disclosure agreements (NDAs) with prospective clients should be in place prior to such submissions, so there usually aren't any issues about showing pieces of work. You always can ask for permission from former clients to show pieces of coding from their projects as marketing tools under NDAs.

If you have a solid résumé and a nice range of samples targeted to the right jobs—ones that you're especially qualified for—then your main challenge is the interview process. As a remote developer, you'll find that nearly all interviews will be conducted via videoconference or phone calls. I've had in-person interviews with local companies, which are a little time consuming but usually okay. Occasionally, an interested employer will fly you to their offices to interview for very large or long-term contracts. This better be worth it, though, because it takes you away from your paid work.

There basically are two types of interviews. One is sort of a formality interview where the project managers or lead developers want to talk just to make sure they're comfortable communicating with you. You probably have the job locked as long as you don't come across as someone they wouldn't want to work with.

The other type of interview is much more technical in nature. That's when you might be asked a bunch of questions about your use of a programming language or to write some code to solve a problem. You might be asked to set up a shared screen so they can see you do the coding or step them through a problem-solving challenge.

Let's face it, technical interviews can be pretty stressful. You are on the spot to sound knowledgeable and often to be able to do some coding on the fly. If you're asked a question that you can't answer, you've got to be able to think on your feet to draw a connection to something you do know or indicate how you have the core skills to address that topic. For example, your response could be something like, "I know about X and Y because they're related, but haven't had the chance to work on Z yet."

Another option is to more directly admit that you don't know the answer and you ask the interviewer(s) for it. Just frame this question in a way that shows how much you're interested in learning and that this is an opportunity you appreciate. Chances are they'll respect your honesty. If the interviewer(s) don't know the answer to their own question, they'll just move on. Don't press them any further or you'll sound like you're trying to embarrass them.

If a project sounds like it will be pushing the boundaries of your skills, you need to be upfront but smart in what you say. What's the most you can say about this topic? Can you show that you have solid depth of knowledge around the topic even if you don't know everything about it? If you get through this part of the interview, you always can do some homework on what's new to you to get the job done.

One thing I've learned having experienced hundreds of interviews is that employers are looking for someone they can depend on to get the job done no matter what. They'd like a programmer with grit and resourcefulness. That means you should be able to tell stories about how you saved the day on projects. What were the challenges and how did you technically and/or creatively address them successfully? Maybe you even can provide a coding sample associated with one of these "overcoming the odds" projects. This really builds their confidence in you beyond your core skills.

Don't be afraid to bring up instances when you asked clients probing questions to reveal avenues to follow for solutions. This reflects your effective communication skills and openness to collaboration. That said, should you ever mention times when you asked for help? That's a little more risky. You want to present yourself as a skilled, independent worker. Therefore, I'd frame this more along the lines of instances when you saw the value in collaborating briefly to address unresolved onboarding or project issues.

Yes, all of this implies that hiring decisions can be as much emotional decisions as technical ones. But remember that these are people who need you to be successful with your work to make them look good. They have their worries, agendas and stressful jobs, so they'll look to you to relieve some of that emotional baggage.

At least some of the stress of being interviewed can be reduced by preparing properly. Familiarize yourself with every detail of the contract description, what's said and isn't said. Make a bullet list of points you think you might need to say regarding the project. Also list points you want to emphasize about your skills, dependability, experience and interest in learning to build on your skills. Reference items like these can be especially valuable if you're a little nervous during interviews.

I like to ask the following question after studying the job description: What does a successful developer for this company and for this role look like? This analysis helps me align with hints they've provided about the project, as well as their culture and work processes.

The human element of the interview process occasionally can lead you to a trap. This has to do with the emotional, cultural or mission aspects with the company. You don't want to get caught up in that. But then again, you also must sound like someone who can fit in enough to establish a productive working relationship. The best you might be able to do in cases like this is to gently steer the conversation back to project description elements.

In any case, I tend to play off cues in the contract description and during the interview to make it more of a two-way conversation. That's so it's not just them asking me questions or testing my skills. After all, they're looking for chemistry as it relates to the process of doing the work, including communication skills.

You can tell that you're having a great interview if you feel like the conversation becomes somewhat informal. It's like you're bonding through shared experiences and some personal connections. This isn't about becoming "friends" as much as it is about building a working business relationship.

On the other end of the interview spectrum, there are the more confrontational ones. This may be where they're really testing you as an outsider. They could have agendas you're not aware of. So the interview serves as a way for them to feel powerful or it's a competitive positioning opportunity for them. These can be red flags about what it might be like to work with them or their team. Don't back out too quickly, though. Chances are that this attitude will fade as the project starts or you can just endure it for the limited time you're working together.

One odd experience I did have with an interviewer had to do with a discussion about Gitflow, the widely accepted workflow model that nearly all of my clients have used. This guy said he didn't like it… period. He described a workflow process he did like—it was his thing. The problem was that his process wasn't supported by the developer community. He showed quite a bit of arrogance to declare that he was right and everyone else is wrong. Imagine starting a working relationship with that issue! Yes, I shrugged it off and completed the project.

A stranger experience I had during an interview was when the manager seemed to be playing some type of psychological game with me. It was as if he wanted me to be more emotional with my answers. His questions obviously were phrased to expose my personality in some way. He even used some pretty bad language and brought up inappropriate stories. I wasn't responding as he wanted and it frustrated him.

Honestly, this was just plain bizarre. I don't know, but maybe he wanted to establish his dominance or leadership over me and other candidates, not just focus on skills and attitudes. Perhaps he wanted to know if I cared enough about the work or would be passionate enough. Again, I got the contract and did the work despite some other business issues that arose to make it a less than pleasant experience.

You might be wondering if I've ever passed on a job because I encountered an exceptionally uncomfortable situation at the interview stage. Actually, no. I always knew what I was getting into and adjusted accordingly. Yes, that means I put up with distractions and an added layer of complexity when it came to communication and processes.

But hey, we all know that many companies are dysfunctional and there are plenty of people who aren't happy in their jobs. If I passed on all of the non-ideal relationship type work, it would be much tougher to keep my revenue high.

Depending upon your level of patience and sanity, a place where you might have to consider passing on a project is if the interviewer is very disrespectful about the value you'll bring to the project. There's also a line you have to draw on what you will accept for hourly rates. If the interviewer keeps knocking down your pay rate to an inappropriate level, then you might want to pass on the contract. Again, I've never had a situation that got that bad.

Negotiations for pay are rare. Most of the time, the pay rate for projects is pre-set and not even discussed. If you are put in the position of negotiating your rate, start with a range that you think is fair and competitive in the marketplace. Never undervalue your skills and what you bring to projects.

That said, accepting lower end pay isn't always a bad thing. It will make it harder for clients to fire you or just end your contract because they'll have a lot of trouble finding someone with equal qualifications to do the job. And you often can increase your margin on such projects by spending less time on them, as long as you still get the work done.

Whether a confrontation occurs about pay or anything else, remember not to take these conflicts personally. They almost all arise from business or culture issues. Maybe you just happen to be dealing with a very unhappy or insecure person. That's life. Just be professional—the adult in the room—to keep things focused on the project.

I think that the keys to successfully landing contract jobs is to do what we all should do when pitching ourselves to employers: Be excited about the job, communicate clearly about our skills and value, and be well-prepared. Getting developer contracts is really about qualifications evidenced by your résumé more than anything else. Because you're selective about applications in the first place, these are contracts that match well with your experience and skills.

I'm decent when it comes to interviews, not necessarily a charismatic speaker or fantastic pitchman. But I always remember that it's sales and we're dealing with humans. You're trying to make a connection because, as I've said, hiring very often is an emotional decision after the skill requirements are met.

Early on, I landed jobs even though I wasn't necessarily the most qualified. Maybe that's even the case now sometimes. What might make the difference is that I convey that I have solid skills, I have a great attitude, I can be trusted to do the work correctly, and I'll be available to them and very responsive during the project.

You'll likely hear back from prospects within a day or two if you got the job. The more time that passes, chances are you weren't a good fit for any number of business or emotionally based reasons. Interestingly, there have been times when I got callbacks several weeks after my interview. Those were cases when their first choice ended up not working out or the project changed in some way and I was the best choice to slip in.

So even when you feel a little discouraged about not landing any contracts for a short period, know that things can turn around in an instant. There are times when too many opportunities come all at once and you have the luxury of selecting the best ones. But if you ever must turn down contracts, be sure to let the staffing agent of contact know that you're always looking for great remote contracts. This will keep you in their prospect system. Of course, you never disclose that you're handling more than one contract at a time.

In the end, hook up with plenty of clients to reach your workload capability. You won't get every contract you apply for. This is why you go after so many projects on an ongoing basis. As long as your batting average is high enough that you achieve your maximum hits (i.e. workload level), strikeouts really don't matter.

Remotely Rich

Chapter 4
Got the Contract... Now What? Onboarding

Onboarding with clients is a time-consuming effort. That means it's a significant investment on your part because there's no way to get around the fact that it takes time away from your other projects. Less time working equals lower revenue.

Just to be clear, onboarding is when you get your development environment set up with clients. You're deepening your understanding about the project, familiarizing yourself with their processes, getting to know the project lead and maybe other team members, clarifying timelines and deliverables, and assessing their expectations. Doing all of this up-front prevents wasted time and energy early in the project.

My main tip regarding onboarding deals with setting up your initial piece of work. It's always best to start a project with a narrow, isolated task—something that's not too connected to many other elements of the project or just plain too large. In other words, begin with a manageable piece such as correcting a bug or working on a micro-feature. This reduces the number of variables within their system to deal with early on and lets you show that you can deliver something solid.

Client expectations play a role in this too. Later I'll get into expectations more, but I need to mention an important lesson I've learned with respect to onboarding. That is to ask where they think they are regarding the parts of the application that have been built already. A unique characteristic about Web development is that clients often have very limited knowledge about what has actually been completed. By asking them for the details, you'll both be able to establish the project's real starting point and ensure that everyone's expectations are realistic.

For example, I had a client ask me why a feature was taking so long to code. He mistakenly believed that it was almost done when I started. The reality was that the feature wasn't even close to being finished when I became involved. I failed to alert him about this, thinking that there must be something I didn't understand at the time. That caused some conflict right off. With some discussion, we resolved the issue. But it did teach me to be candid about any lurking suspicions or concerns right off the bat when I start a project. Clear the air immediately to prevent trouble down the road with client expectations.

Onboarding also is when you want to get up to speed on the meaning of terminology clients use. That not only includes technical terminology related to the code-base but also relevant business/industry terminology they use. This is your a chance to gain context about the code you'll be writing and problem solving, as well as visualize patterns in processes. You want the elements of the project to come together in your mind so you have a comfortable understanding about the big picture or overall structure of the project.

The best way to avoid getting overwhelmed by trying to handle too much at first is by learning a bit at a time about all of this. So again, this comes back to tackling a small piece of the project initially. You want an opportunity to deliver value quickly and make a good impression.

Sadly though, a smooth onboarding process isn't the reality for how typical projects start. Clients tend to want to begin projects from scratch. For example, they want you to develop a complete design right out of the gate. That opens the opportunity for too many questions to go unanswered and for a large number of factors to be unaddressed. This results in frustrating false starts, delays in producing deliverables and chances for misunderstandings about your skills or project management.

The best prevention strategy is for you to propose what you want to do to launch the project based on your professional experience. It's not difficult to make a pretty compelling argument for starting small, building efficiencies, supporting timeframes, establishing clarity about the project, etc. Anything that saves time, effort and money should interest clients.

Another important lesson I've learned is not to be afraid to ask for help or, to phrase it slightly differently, ask to discuss important questions that have come up. If you don't understand certain aspects of a project, terminology, steps in their processes, communication channels or other things, just ask. No question is stupid. In fact, managers usually appreciate your desire for clarity to prevent you from spinning your wheels trying to figure everything out on your own. It's just too costly for them and you. Often, your questions address points you couldn't have known as an outside contractor who is new to the company. You even might be bringing up questions that others who worked on the project were afraid to ask or didn't know to ask.

Try not to lead into your questions with something like, "I'm totally confused about this…" or "I'm lost and I need you to explain…" Be professional and specific to show that you know how to get answers through collaboration so you can move forward. For example, you could frame a question this way: "I was taking at look at the terminology connected with function X and I'd like some explanations to make sure I code this correctly." So plan out how you'd like to ask your questions so you don't lose credibility with the client.

Here's another really important point about onboarding. You definitely don't want to conduct more than one onboarding process at a time. There's considerable real-time communication with the client and labor-intensive front-end effort on your part. And onboarding always takes place during normal work hours, which pushes your other work to early mornings, late afternoons and evenings. Onboarding can involve a lot to keep straight in your head while maintaining your necessary level of work on existing projects to keep your income flowing.

If you do face simultaneous onboarding for a couple of projects just by unfortunate chance, find a creative way to delay one or minimize the process. For example, you could propose to start an easy part of the work to "get your feet wet" with it and then cover most of the onboarding afterward.

You also might be able to take advantage of a temporarily

lightened or delayed onboarding load if you must wait for system access, requirements, prerequisite meetings, etc. You also could find other ways to spread out onboarding for one project while you dive in deeply on the other to shorten that process.

Anything you can do to speed your understanding of the project and everything else connected to it, the better. Every client and project is different so it's tough to devise general streamlining strategies for onboarding. But at least you know that you'll eventually reach a milestone a fairly short way into the project when onboarding turns into a normal work mode.

There have been a couple of times during onboarding when my client was very busy and the process on their end dragged everything out quite a bit. Once I was brought onboard and couldn't get access to their system. I was being paid to wait for them to get things in order so I could start working. This is what can happen in cases when they fail to get a computer to you that they want you to use, you don't have a VPN token, or there's an orientation meeting you must wait to attend. In a way, these delays can be nice since you're being paid to wait and can focus on other client's projects.

A down side to this can occur as well. One huge trap when onboarding is if clients simply hand off some documentation for you read. They expect you to glean an exemplary understanding of their systems based on the writings from a previous contractor who is probably no longer working with the company for a reason. Don't let them toss you into a dark room, sliding tidbits under the door here and there, while only conversing with you to check on your progress. You must take command with these people and extract the information that you need to move forward on the real work.

I've probably experienced about everything that can happen during the onboarding and project launch processes. A somewhat painful example that comes to mind was when I was hired to use Python to create a Web site. They didn't use any development package, just straight Python. Without getting into all of the technical details, their desire basically was to have data saved into files instead of a database. Let's just say their expectations were highly unconventional and problematic right from the start.

Needless to say, it took me a while just to figure out their expectations on how to accomplish what they wanted to do they way they wanted it done. Steep learning curves are costly in time requirements. So this process took way too much of my time. Add to this the fact that they established a totally unrealistic one-month deadline.

I know that I couldn't have anticipated any of this during onboarding, including how dysfunctional communication was within the team. The project went on to take far more time than I had planned—there were some long nights working on this. I had to manage my other projects quite differently just to keep all of the balls in the air.

This is a great example of being tough, to stick with a very difficult project to the very end. At times, the project could have been seen as impossible based on everything being overly complicated. But that's when I learned to step up, have confidence in my skills and get the work done. I kept the prize—the revenue—in mind to serve as my motivation.

Getting the job launched and done from the onboarding stage sometimes can take a surprising turn in other ways. I was hired by a Fortune 100 company to build an upgraded certification training Web site. As we moved forward with the project, I discovered that they didn't have any version controls. There could have been any number of people working on various parts of this project and no one would have known what anyone else was doing. This introduced a huge potential source for errors and complexity.

The project just couldn't proceed with any efficiency and quality control unless we established a version control process. That's right, I ended up training everyone on version control even though I wasn't hired to do that. It turned out that this caused some issues with working relationships and internal politics.

I actually never got the chance to do any programming due to this diversion. My involvement with the project ended after the version control set-up was complete but not fully implemented. This is just another case of how you might not have any way of knowing what you're getting into with projects until you start.

So just to recap about onboarding, be prepared for surprises but try to keep the onboarding process as efficient as possible. Don't be afraid to direct the process as much as you can to fit your preferences. Clients usually are impressed when you take the initiative as a "consulting" project manager to get work going quickly and avoid complications or delays. If unexpected issues arise, make that an opportunity to show your flexibility and resourcefulness in guiding the client toward solutions.

Chapter 5
Golden Rules

I contend that there are five golden rules to establish and maintain a $450,000 per year developer business.

Rule #1: Stick to the 40-hour billing target.
You are securing full-time jobs as a developer. That means your employer is expecting 40 hours worth of work from you, no matter how long it takes you to do the job. As I've said, my experience is that you can complete those 40 hours of work in around 20 hours if you work efficiently using solid core skills.

I strongly suggest that you avoid billing over 40 hours to kick into overtime. This is because overtime screams to your client that you may be working too slowly or are not as skilled as you originally indicated. Billing less than 40 hours might make it appear that you don't deserve full-time status. Your client could think that you should be assigned more work to fill those available hours or the time required to do the original work was overestimated so your time should be should scaled back.

These scenarios will dismantle your $450,000 per year strategy. You've got to stay under your employer's radar by delivering the expected amount of work on time and as a 40 per week effort. So even if you work over or under the normal 20 hours per week, bill that 40 hours because everything will balance out over the life of the contract.

This natural balancing of your time also applies across the weekly workflow of your three concurrent projects. There'll be heavy work times and lighter times with each contract. You may be surprised about how your total workload will stay quite manageable over time because three different schedules rarely spike and drop at the same time. And the more efficiently you do the work, the more flexible your daily or weekly schedule will be.

Rule #2: Always be in marketing mode.
You never know when projects will be delayed, unexpectedly terminated or just finished ahead of schedule. You've got to be in the running for new contracts all the time to prevent revenue killing workload gaps. There also could be times when you don't win contracts, so other ones should be in the works.

Be ready to replace existing contracts quickly by constantly applying for new ones. Small projects can be great to fill in workload gaps, so don't automatically dismiss those. You never know when quick projects will be extended or lead to new, larger ones.

I urge you to commit to spending some time each day marketing your services by searching for leads, submitting your résumé and following up appropriately. I can't stress enough how important this is. Being lazy about your marketing will cost you big-time. Even if you've been able to rely on staffing agencies calling regularly with jobs, you just can't count on them doing all of your prospecting work for you.

Rule #3: Get your hours approved weekly.
It's critical that you get your work hours approved every week. This is the industry standard. You might unintentionally assume some big risks on getting paid if you don't do this.

For example, I had a client who thought I was working way too slowly. They expected the work to be completed in three days but it took four weeks. The reasons for the slow pace were their unrealistic expectations and coding issues that arose during the project—their fault, not mine. When the deadline hit, low and behold they didn't want to pay me. Luckily, I was careful to get my hours approved each week which represented their incremental approvals. I did get paid, but they weren't happy.

By the way, once your hours are approved incrementally by clients most staffing agencies are on the hook to pay you even if they encounter problems getting paid by those clients.

Rule #4: Act like a professional.
You, as a developer, are in the service business. You won't be in business long unless you communicate and work with clients in a professional manner. This includes how you deal with agencies that coordinate contracts with your clients. Good relationships with agencies and, more specifically, their placement representatives are vital to having them do a significant portion of your prospecting for you.

The most important business relationships are with your clients because you want them all to be as long-term as possible. Other than providing top quality work and delivering work on time, the following are a things you can do to come across as a professional:

- **Status calls** – A daily (morning) project status call builds trust and keeps the communication lines open with clients. It only takes a couple of minutes to update your clients on what you're doing, address questions or resolve challenges. If you don't have any project details to provide, just "check in" and say that the project is moving along well and on-schedule.

  In all of your communications with clients, you have to avoid vague or incomplete answers to their questions. They'll tend to assume that you understand what's going on and build erroneous expectations based on that. So respond clearly and completely. If they send you a message or leave one by phone, respond very quickly with direct answers.

- **Work records** – Almost all of your clients will ask you to log into their system to record your hours each day. Like clockwork, I log into the system in the morning to show that I'm online and at work. They rarely monitor your work activity but this habit is another way to show that you're reliable. It's true that you'll actually be juggling several projects and even working odd hours. However, clients want to see that you're working full-time business days for them.

- **Meetings** – As a remote worker, nearly all of your "meetings" will be online or by conference call. You want to maintain good attendance with these to show that you're an enthusiastic member of the team. If you have points to contribute, it might be efficient for you to jot them down prior to the meeting to ensure that they are covered.

Too often, meetings turn into chat sessions about subjects not relevant to the project. Sometimes I can get work done while the others talk so it's not a total waste of time. If the vital subjects have been covered already, you can respectfully say that you really want to get back to work and must exit the meeting. One more suggestion: Take some notes during the meeting about what needs to be done that day or in the next few days and mention those talking points at the next meeting. This reflects how you're right on top of things and focused on the project.

This talk about meetings reminds me about a very awkward incident related to a team conference call a while back. I joined a call after it started and a participant didn't know I was on the line. He started bad-mouthing me to everybody, saying that I took credit for his work. I couldn't stay silent and sharply corrected him. In fact, I read my previous email to him for everyone to hear. In it I clearly gave him credit and suggested that everyone follow his good work. He never apologized.

- **Deliverables** – It's simple, just deliver quality work on time. That's what your clients care about the most. That's the service a seasoned developer provides.

- **Conflicts** – There always will be some conflicts in business relationships. These can range from personality conflicts with managers to disagreements due to miscommunications about project tasks. It's not in your best interests to get upset or say something you'll regret when conflicts arise. Just solve the problem and move on. Be the adult in the room, showing that you want to work things out to complete the job successfully for everyone's sake.

  This also goes for how you react during calls, meetings and through emails or text messages. If you're upset about something, take a time out to calm down before responding. I guarantee that this attitude will prevent a lot of stress.

- **Availability** – A client who knows he/she can reach you even beyond business hours usually is a very happy client. This communication could involve a problem that's come up or just reflect a need for some reassurance that a phase of the project is going well.

  It really doesn't take that much effort to be a responsive team member. The benefits in building trust and professional respect are significant. I've told fellow developers many times that I like to position myself to make my clients look good. I'm there for them when they need me.

Rule #5: Strive for working in a coasting pattern.
I describe coding and problem solving in your sweet spot as working in a coasting pattern. It's the type of work you do so well that it's almost second nature. This is when you can work very quickly and efficiently, accomplishing tasks in the least amount of

time. You want to reach this stage as rapidly as possible on the majority of your projects.

Most often, this mainly is a function of selecting projects that are right in your wheelhouse of skills. I wish I always could get these projects every time, but odds are projects that are a perfect fit will only be a portion of your overall work. You can increase the number of projects that offer long coasting patterns by expanding your skill set. Building deep knowledge in an extra area or two can pay off big time.

Another way to experience a great coasting pattern is to know early on—ideally at the interview or onboarding stage—that the base system for the project is high quality. That means your contract to develop an add-on feature will be far easier to crank out. This also may be the case with a small build for a minimum viable product versus a huge build. Characteristics of these projects should scream "maximum efficiency" to you.

Remotely Rich

Chapter 6
The 1099 Versus W-2 Mentality

Achieving success as a remote developer has a lot to do with your mindset. I call this the 1099 versus W-2 mentality. It's very important that you shift your perspective on work to the 1099 side because it's way different than having a "regular" job.

First off, let's define what I'm talking about from a terminology standpoint. An independent contractor (IRS 1099 filer) pays his/her own taxes and is not considered an employee of companies it serves. An employee (IRS W-2 filer) has taxes taken out of his/her salary by the employer and is subject to all of its (in-house) employment policies.

The mindset of a 1099 contractor is based on a desire to control his/her time, working environment, work location and income potential. It's about freedom and control. You've got to want to start your own company and provide contract services to clients to earn $450,000 a year as I outline in this book.

But what about the security of working for some big company? Get over it. Just look at employment statistics in the U.S. for the software industry and you'll see that job security is a myth. Yes, there's a regular paycheck and sometimes decent benefits like health insurance. But working independently as a contractor offers you unlimited earnings and you can buy the benefits you need. You can enjoy this without the fear of being laid off due to outsourcing, learning that the company was sold and may be restructured, or seeing the company mismanaged into failure. Doesn't a work life without those fears sound more like security?

Beyond the obvious employment factors like these, another area related to mindset regards your relationships with managers and project teams. A W-2 employee potentially is permanently stuck with the manager and team he/she is hired to work with. A 1099 contractor knows the project has a life and even difficult relationships with managers or teams eventually will pass. If in the highly unusual situation of a business relationship being intolerable, you can terminate the contract to move on to other contracts without the loss of your sole source of income.

Oh yes, office politics, power struggles and personal agendas also can make W-2 employment miserable. Think of how much time is wasted on these distractions every day by full-time employees at companies. It's no wonder that you as a 1099 contractor can accomplish 40 hours of work in half that time just by not working in that environment.

That said, I admit that you do want to be a part of internal business politics to a limited degree just to be engaged with team members. There can be a disconnect by working remotely as a 1099 contractor. You must consciously look for ways to show your passion for the job, how things are done and your commitment to the best interests of the company.

There's no escaping an element of office politics when doing this. Connecting with team members within the ecosystem—via shared experiences—of office politics can help build better relationships that result in more contracting opportunities. The key is to stay as far away as you can from getting into personal issues or conflicts. Personal stuff is poison and can put your contracts at risk even if you do outstanding work.

Internal communication can be another challenge within this mindset. When you're a W-2 employee in an office with team members, you have unlimited opportunities for planned and spontaneous communication about projects. You likely know if you're performing up to everyone's expectations and what they think of you. Working remotely as a 1099 contractor, you just won't have that same level of communication.

This introduces some risk of you being considered "the outsider." Issues could arise that make it convenient for employees to use you as the fall guy. But honestly, the chances of this occurring are minimal especially if you make an effort to build good communication channels with team members.

So a 1099 contractor mindset essentially means that you must learn how to think like an independent service vendor and not as an employee with a job. You need to be resourceful in finding ways to overcome the disconnects of working remotely to build solid working relationships with clients. Your position may be the front line service provider as a developer, but you'll also wear the hat of a salesperson, customer relations manager, marketing specialist and CEO. That sounds more intimidating than it is, as it's just a matter of maintaining a priority of providing great customer service.

Chapter 7
Setting up Your Business and Protecting Yourself

Welcome to the world of self-employment as an independent developer.

I did some homework before starting my business to make sure I did it right. It's very important that you too set up your business correctly to prevent tax or legal issues down the road.

Understand that I'm not a business start-up expert and am not providing a comprehensive description of everything you may need to do to set up your business. Your best approach is to consult an attorney, startup advisor, accountant, relevant government agencies and others. I'm just covering some key points from my own experience switching from a W-2 employee to a 1099 independent contractor.

Business structure
You should do some research or consult with an expert to select the right business structure. This selection affects your exposure to personal liability, the type of taxes you pay and reporting,

certain accounting requirements, and other business factors. I've heard of developers incorporating as C corporations, Sub-chapter S corporations, limited liability companies (LLC) or even B (benefit) corporations. I think the most common structures are Sub-chapter S and LLCs. Large companies and government agencies typically require that you are incorporated, so a sole proprietorship may not be a good choice.

Lots of free or low cost help is available from small business centers, community college workshops, entrepreneur associations and start-up centers. Even incubators and co-working facilities offer guidance for resident businesses if you choose that route.

Licenses and registrations
License and registration requirements vary with cities, counties and states. If you're operating in a city, you may need to apply for a city business license or permit. Some counties might require registration or some type of license/permit. States require you to file your articles of incorporation, business name or "doing business as" name, and possibly other registrations.

Federal rules mainly regard IRS requirements. You must register your business with the IRS to obtain an Employer Identification Number (EIN) for tax reporting purposes. Many states have very helpful business start-up guides online and processes to streamline the steps to create businesses.

Accountants, lawyers and business advisors can help with the paperwork. It's important that you do this correctly or you could be subject to fines or penalties.

Taxes and reporting

Depending upon the type of company structure you adopt, you will need to deal with state and federal payroll taxes (when your company pays you), quarterly estimates or reporting, federal unemployment tax, and annual business tax filings. There also could be property tax due on business property that you own, such as computer equipment, especially if you set up a separate office. A good accountant can advise you about all taxes and reporting. I have an accountant who handles all of this for me.

Accounting and invoicing

Your accounting and client invoicing tasks shouldn't be all that complicated. Business accounting procedures for a one-person operation are fairly simple to handle yourself. You basically need to record all income and expenses in detail, so tax reporting and end-of-year return filing is accurate. Again, I prefer to have my accountant deal with this so I can focus on working to earn more money.

Invoicing is only a task to manage if you work directly with clients. A nice benefit of working through staffing agencies is that they do all of the invoicing of clients that they connect you with. By the way, even though clients typically use online systems to track my hours worked I like to keep my own record so I know where I stand on earnings and trends. This also allows me double check reports from clients to make sure their numbers are correct.

Business expenses

If you're self-employed, you definitely need to keep accurate records of all business expenses for tax purposes. You don't want to lose out on legitimate deductions because you failed to keep receipts, credit card statements and other documentation. So don't forget to hang onto all business expense receipts, either digitally or as paper copies, as proof if questions arise.

Nearly everything that you pay for to operate your business counts as an expense. This includes Internet service, equipment, phone, Web hosting, rent/office space, office supplies, furniture, insurance, utilities (a portion of utilities for a home office), all costs associated with contractors or employees you have, and all business travel including car mileage or mass transit fees.

Expenses also include professional fees from your accountant, lawyer, etc., commissions you pay to marketing services, business related online and other subscriptions, and many more line items. Your accountant should be able to advise you on an efficient recordkeeping method and applicable business expenses to track.

I'd recommend that you get a business credit card to prevent mixing personal and business charges. Most business cards provide itemized year-end summaries of all expenses by typical IRS categories. I prefer to pay off all credit card charges each month to prevent paying high interest rates.

Insurance
The type and amounts of business insurance you need to get mainly are dictated by clients. They often specify certain coverage types and dollar levels in their contracts.

You'll probably need to buy a general business policy with liability coverage. This is especially important if you have a separate office, but even if you work from home. The reason for this is because you'll have a legitimate business operation going, business equipment and at least some dedicated space for your work. Also, it's assumed that you might meet with clients there, even though that's very rare for developers.

Consider checking into what's called professional insurance such as "errors and omissions" coverage if additional liability protection makes sense or is required by certain employers. That said, programming is an iterative process so it's not like you have major liability associated with delivering a final complete product with no ongoing approvals. If the final product doesn't work, you should have plenty of milestone approvals to protect you.

Although you might be young, in great health or just feel invulnerable, health insurance is a very good idea. A bad accident or illness could wipe out a big chunk of your savings. I don't know much about disability insurance. That's the type where you can protect part of your income if an injury or illness prevents you from working for a period. This might be smart if you have a family and are the sole breadwinner or have significant financial liabilities to cover each month.

Business bank account

So you can get paid and pay bills, you must open a business bank account. Personal finances and business income and expenses really should be kept separate, especially for tax and legal reasons. You'll need to provide your EIN, incorporation papers, business address, contact information, personal ID and possibly proof of government licenses and registrations to open an account.

Usually the simplest type of a business checking account is more than adequate for a developer's needs. This will cut down on fees charged by your bank. If you start to maintain a large balance in the account, many banks offer interest-bearing accounts. The interest rate rarely is good so you'd be better off lowering the balance by transferring funds to higher earning investments or retirement accounts. An independent investment advisor can help you with this to make sure you make educated decisions.

Getting paid
As I mentioned previously, staffing agencies handle all invoicing for you and typically pay you by direct deposit to your business bank account. Another benefit of working through staffing agencies is that they'll make sure you're paid even if the client is slow or fails to pay. You might be paid by check from companies that you work with directly, but most now use direct deposit too.

You could be given an option to be paid via a payment service such as PayPal, but they charge you a percentage each time. That can be quite costly over time. I guess if you're given no choice on this it would be tolerable but maybe this requirement should be one of your non-negotiable items.

Paying yourself
There are two main ways you can pay yourself: one is by establishing a regular weekly or monthly salary and the other is to just pay yourself various amounts when you want to. It's easiest to use electronic transfer between your business account

and personal account, but some developers still write paychecks to themselves.

It's a good idea to make sure there's always enough money in your business account to cover taxes and near-term or surprise business expenses, so don't pay yourself every dime in the account. Sometimes you could let the account balance get a little lower than normal when you know a deposit will be made by a client within a day or so. Just be careful because you don't want to have to transfer funds from your personal account, as a business loan, to cover a pending expense.

Work in an office or at home?

Choosing to work in a separate office or your home is an important decision. An office adds potentially significant operating costs, but it's considered a business expense for tax purposes and you have a dedicated work environment available.

A home office is very convenient and cost-effective but you must have the discipline and necessary privacy to work there. Note that if you have space dedicated to your business such as a separate room, that probably can be claimed as a deduction on your taxes. Either way, you need a fast Internet connection, decent coverage for your cell phone and a comfortable work area.

I have a separate office close to home. It just fits my work style. But popular new options for start-ups and some remote contract services are co-working offices and incubator type office spaces. The additional services some offer can be worthwhile but you may lose a certain amount of privacy and there can be a bunch of distractions. If you do decide that you want to work from home, check your neighborhood codes, covenants and restrictions (CC&Rs) and local zoning—or if in a condo, your owner's association—to make sure a business in your home is legal.

The outside office versus home office decision really comes down more to personal factors and work style than anything else. That is, unless you choose to have contractors or employees on-site part-time or full-time. It can be uncomfortable to have them in your home and might complicate things like insurance coverage.

Communications and accessibility
To separate business from personal matters, you might want to get a separate business phone number. The extra cost is a legitimate business expense. Do clients care whether they're calling a personal versus business line? No, but personal and business calls may conflict at times.

It's also a good idea to establish a business email address, preferably with your own domain name as that reflects a more established business. And for marketing purposes, a simple Web site is a good idea. Basically repurpose the key information from your résumé and typical cover letters as marketing language on the site.

You might get some value from a thoughtfully composed LinkedIn page if you put some effort into building a network of industry contacts, customers and colleagues over time. There are other networking sites that could help you build some direct connections with potential clients and increase your visibility in the marketplace. How much time you spend on these sites depends on your marketing preferences and if you think they would help with your credibility among staffing agencies.

The other communication tool I find very convenient is Skype. If you don't have an account, I recommend getting one. It's great for conference calls and meetings when they aren't coordinated via services your clients use.

Résumé and samples

There are plenty of examples of great résumés for service providers like developers, both online and in books. I just suggest that you keep it up-to-date with your skills, programming languages you know and include keywords you see in job descriptions. Also, put together a small collection of work samples to show off your best work and range of skills.

One additional marketing tool that may be worth preparing is a capabilities statement. They're needed more often for government agencies but can be valuable for large companies too. Look online for examples and guidelines. If you're not familiar at all with capabilities statements, they usually include the following for service businesses: a paragraph describing your business, your core competencies, a list of your showcase clients, any differentiators (special skills/value you offer), NAICS and class codes, and complete contact information.

Non-disclosure agreement (NDA)

Staffing agencies and clients almost always provide NDAs for you to sign to protect them and you. However, startups or very small businesses that you might contract with directly may not have NDAs prepared. You can find examples and templates online or get one drafted by an attorney if the need arises.

Saving your money
Unless you spend everything you earn, which is not very sustainable, you'll want to save money for future use and retirement. I'm a believer in investing in myself first, professionally and in my business. That includes everything from owning the right technologies to make my work efficient to getting massages that counter the effects stress. Beyond that, save money however you feel comfortable. That includes investment and retirement accounts. The right savings strategy can reduce your taxes and provide long-term security when you want to work less.

Disclaimer

The information contained in this chapter should not be considered expert business, accounting or legal advice. It was based on personal experience and is accurate to the best of my knowledge. I strongly recommend that you seek professional advice when setting up your business and for ongoing guidance.

Chapter 8
Working Remotely

The critical part of earning $450,000 a year is to work remotely. It's the only way you can have three "full-time" jobs simultaneously. There is a method to this madness.

Morning is my communication time with clients. I check in and provide updates. And I log onto their systems to indicate that I'm starting work. The other important part of my morning routine is to review and update my checklist of action items for the day. If something makes the list, it absolutely must be done that day. No excuses, no compromise, no matter how late I must work. The checklist includes communication with clients, specific project tasks, marketing actions, staffing agency duties/follow-up, communication with or submissions to my accountant, and other business operation responsibilities.

Other than devoting the necessary time to marketing, the balance of my day is spent coding and problem solving. It depends on my workload and project schedules as to how much time I'll spend on each project. There are times when I only work on one project all day; other times, I'll split the day fairly evenly among the three projects.

Remotely Rich

During times when I have a particularly heavy workload, I'll work evenings and right through weekends. I try not to pull all-nighters but there definitely have been some marathon coding sessions into the morning hours. This may have occurred because of deadlines, but also because I just got on a roll and didn't want to kill my momentum or train of thought.

Does this work life sound pretty intense? It is. But it's under my control. You could say that the tendency behind this control over my time is based on selfishness. In a way, that's true. I've made a commitment for now to maintain a certain work-life imbalance—almost everything outside of work comes second.

To establish this amount of focus, you have to ask, "What is wasting my time?" and then eliminate it. This might include having a beer with a buddy, going to a film with a friend or loved one, surfing the Internet, watching TV or even grocery shopping. Yes, there are plenty of occasions when I'll just order food for delivery so I don't waste my time going to a restaurant or the store. All of this potentially wasted time must be spent working so that I earn the big bucks.

I won't sugarcoat the issues that can surface. It's tough to get people you care about to understand your priorities. Relationships tend to suffer. So how much you work—and how much you earn—is based on the priorities you set.

Programming day and night requires isolation, unless you're extremely focused and can do it with distractions around you. And speaking of isolation, the reality is that I rarely even talk with clients these days, even with morning updates or check-ins.

It's mostly done by text messaging with occasional brief Skype meetings. Working remotely at an intense level is what I call working in a virtualized world, without much contact with others on many days.

You basically need to find ways to minimize your involvement with clients' use of phone calls and meetings of any kind as long as you maintain the right level of customer service. I've actually proposed less communication-driven processes to clients to set up things the way I prefer to work. When that wasn't an option, I've dropped off meeting calls once I gave my update and there were no questions.

The shorter the morning calls and messages about projects to managers and team members, the better. I always have a bunch of tasks to take care of in the morning. So I have to be extremely efficient to ensure that I maximize my time to do the actual work I've been hired to do.

I should mention something here about project milestones and deadlines for projects because they are the workflow drivers for programming remotely. More times than not, I'm hired while clients are still devising development plans. Clients often rely on me for estimates on when pieces of the project can be delivered and the related process steps.

Clients typically employ Agile's methodology called "backlog grooming." It's a way to explain what it will take to do the work along the way and complete it. There also are times when there's a drop-dead final delivery date for a project and clients work backwards from that. I'm expected to provide guidance for that too. As a remote "outsider" who likely has a clearer view of projects than in-house employees, I'm usually valued for a realistic perspective on workflow.

One side note about Agile methodologies. Agile and working remotely on multiple contracts are not very compatible. Do everything you can to minimize your involvement with Agile because the associated activities can take too much time away from work.

Here's one of the great perks about working remotely. With a decent Internet connection available, you can work from nearly anywhere. I've hit the road for weeklong trips to pretty nice locations and taken my work with me. The change of environment can be very refreshing and stimulating. I believe getting away fairly regularly is a way to counter the stress of working long hours and reduce the negative effects of all that isolation. Of course, never disclose to clients that you're sitting by the pool at a resort or holed up at a mountain lodge.

I've occasionally gotten more than I bargained for on getaway work retreats. For example, I checked into a Southern California hotel one time on a getaway. I thought I reserved a simple hotel room but it turned out to be some kind of love nest themed room. Oh man, it had a spinning orange mirror in the middle of the room and decorations that were way too kinky.

I didn't have time to find another place to stay so I was there for three nights, Hey, it did have a nice pool and other decent amenities. None of this proved to be all that big of a distraction because I hardly left the room. I had a lot of work to do. A slight regret is that I continually ordered room service so I didn't need to spend time in restaurants. That was one expensive food bill at the end.

Whether you're working remotely in the office, at home or somewhere on the road, the key is to be goal oriented. The top-level objective is to maximize income by working multiple projects and providing good value to clients. Related goals may be paying off debt, saving a large chunk of money, sacrificing and working very hard for a period to be able to ease off at a target date, or even building the foundation of a scalable business.

What's your goal and can you imagine how working remotely can get you there? Give this some thought while you consider the financial upside.

Before I close out this topic of working remotely, I must admit that some of my most enjoyable projects have involved in-house work. Sorry if that sounds contradictory to the theme of this book. The truth is that I enjoyed the more tangible aspects of seeing my work put to use in the operation of work at companies. Working remotely, we move on after finishing projects and never see the sites or systems being used by intended audiences. But as enjoyable as those projects were, I knew very well that they severely limited my earnings potential. I'd rather have the money.

Remotely Rich

Chapter 9
Managing Client Expectations

I've talked a little about client expectations in previous chapters. However, I want to focus in on a few points and examples here because expectations can have a huge impact of your workflow and relationships with clients.

First off, what could be at the heart of a client's biggest set of expectations at the start of the project? I'm talking about an expectation that 100% of my clients have had.

It's that they believe that the quality of the code they've developed so far and now are handing off to me is in perfect or at least in excellent condition. So when I'm tasked with adding modules to their system, they expect everything to work perfectly upon delivery from me.

The fact is that 100% of them are wrong. Things are never, ever what they seem at the start of about any size project.

You've got to assume that just about all code contains erroneous instructions, redundant code, defunct code, unrecognized potential incompatibilities and even missing code. There are so many explanations related to this situation. Clients may not know how many developers have worked on it with their own quality controls, how accurately they wrote it, how many shortcuts were taken due to pressure on developers to finish quickly, how internal politics or agendas affected the development, how many bugs were overlooked, how well the system was thought out from a design standpoint, or how many components were never completely finished.

Project managers assume everything is good because it's their job to vouch for the project. To admit the coding flaws would result in potentially looking incompetent, revealing shortcomings in their processes or making managers' and stakeholders' project decisions appear faulty. Yes, ignorance can be bliss for these managers and even their entire teams.

In cases when I'm hired to develop systems from scratch, another set of client expectations comes into play. Managers have time and cost estimates in their heads, based on guesses or marketing decisions—or who knows what.

A detailed design plan might have been created but it's probably unrealistic when it comes to project execution. The end product might not have been thought through enough in-depth to anticipate the need for additional modules or functions. Often, managers think the project details are set in stone knowing in their hearts that many changes are inevitable.

Your best option in these cases is to manage client expectations right from the start, whether you'll be coding new modules or creating entirely new systems. Offer your assessment of the project based on evidence you see in the plans or in the existing code.

I admit that this is very challenging on completely new projects because you're talking about something that doesn't exist yet. But you can look at the information they give you and use your experience with similar projects as a guide about assumptions, errors in thinking, faulty estimates, etc. Also, you'll likely have to get into the project to a certain degree to determine if existing code is actually compatible with the new modules you've been tasked to create.

Here's an example of this I recently encountered. I was hired to add some functions to an application. One involved adding a dropdown list of options that wasn't supposed to include the currently selected option. Think of settings for the language used by an application, with the default as English. They didn't want English to show up on the drop-down list.

In cases like this, the application must know what the current language is to determine what not to include in the list, right? But the application couldn't determine which option not to show. The client and I expected that it was pretty simple to add this one little function. But it was way more complicated because there was a bug in the existing application they handed off to me that wouldn't let the options be set properly. The client wasn't happy to hear that the application was broken and that fixing it would require more time and work.

A wildcard in this expectation game is your assessment of how well your project manager or development team will accept critical feedback. Sometimes they'll welcome your feedback if it's backed up with enough evidence and presented as "in the best interests of the team" to achieve success.

Other times, pointing out problems will make clients very defensive and even angry. In any case, it helps if you show confidence in your knowledge, skills and assessment. Assume a position of respectful authority based on your expertise. If you sound timid, they'll question your skills and accuracy of your judgment.

Another issue related to expectations is about being a hero. I've tried to be a hero on projects far too many times. You know, work beyond the call of duty to correct problems to save the day while not disclosing how bad things are. It has rarely paid off. The stress and unpaid extra hours weren't worth it. There have been times when I called out the manager only to have my skills or attitude questioned. I suggest avoiding the hero mode.

A compromise position is to point out the type or number of issues that you think will be accepted by the client. You do your best to balance honesty with surrender (to the level of flaws in the project). Maybe a little heroism is worth blending with the reality that the quality of your work may be questioned at no fault of your own.

The key is to disclose enough to the client as concerns or suspicions arise so that you've provided fair warning about the risks to the quality of the end product. Even if you do this, your skills may be questioned because it's far easier for them to blame you for problems than anyone else on the client's team.

Of course, the extreme situation is when you just let the fires burn. That's when the project is a complete mess from the start and there is little you can do to save it. Your strategy might be to communicate what you can about the problems and keep working away on the elements that are most manageable as the project plummets to the ground. You might be blamed for the crash and burn… or not.

The nice thing about being a contractor is that you can walk away if necessary. And don't kick yourself for not seeing disasters coming. You can't always see fatal signs while onboarding.

Then there are expectations regarding the amount of time required to do the job. Clients more often than not have totally unrealistic timeframes for projects. This often originates from the top people in companies and then pressures managers below. Programming always takes longer than expected because of inadequate preparation of the requirements, scope creep for what clients want accomplished and problems identified along the way.

For example, they might expect coding of a module to be finished in one week. It makes you wonder if an educated estimate was ever made for the work. Or perhaps someone just thought a challenging deadline would motivate a developer to rise to the occasion. In these cases, the work just can't be finished by the deadline. Either the client accepts the reality that more time is needed—possibly aided by your initial warning about inadequate time—or questions your skills.

It's possible that a rock star level programmer could figure out in advance that it will take one thing or another to do the job in cases like this. There are those with extraordinary levels of programming expertise who seem to be able to assess everything from the starting point to the completed project to determine time requirements. Most of us just can't predict the future like that so we have to do our best to estimate requirements based on past projects and some educated guesses. We just hope that managers will listen and understand.

This brings me to scope creep. The task list for projects always grows as work proceeds despite clients' expectations to the contrary. Once the initial project is shaping up well, clients tend to see related features or functions that would be helpful to add. Also, "while your working under the hood" new tasks always seem to arise. This usually involves fixing some known bugs or tweaking some code to make a function work better. Make sure that clients properly document these requests to ensure that you'll be covered for permission to fix them and payment for that work.

Another type of situation when expectations end up out of line is when a project is running behind or in trouble. A manager is told to call in additional, usually contract, resources to keep the work on track. It's like ordering firefighters to run into a burning building. But in the case of programming, throwing more resources at a project often backfires into an even worse situation.

When this has happened to me, I've had to be the poor soul who gets to alert the team that the situation is even worse than they thought. On the other hand, the fresh eyes of a new programmer can be just the trick to catch what others didn't see or get that key function or module up and running. Programming triage isn't for the faint of heart but it is a bit of a rush to dive into the chaos and bring some order to it all.

My advice is to provide plenty of scenarios about what might happen as you start to work on the project. Such "fair warning" protects you from a certain amount of criticism down the road and prepares the client for the realities of managing disasters. This isn't so much about trying to be a hero as it is being the calm director who makes a situation at least a little more manageable for everyone.

This situation also brings up a scenario that's quite common. It's when clients expect you to add or fix something without following industry best practices. I've been told to just "hack it together" in a way that the clients want. I always warn them that the hack might work but it could cause unintended incompatibilities with other code or become an anomaly later that sets up additional functionality issues.

The challenge is that to do the work the right way it may take additional time and cost more. So it's a decision point for clients. You've fulfilled your responsibility by expressing your concerns so don't feel guilty if you must proceed following the client's wishes.

I should mention that clients' expectations could be affected by what's said during the interview and onboarding processes. Clients often assume that you know everything about programming related to their projects. They never want contractors to be paid for learning on the job. So it's just best to say that you can do the job. Don't say anything about liking challenges or ramping up quickly. That type of talk implies that you'll need to learn something, which results in clients thinking that you can be paid less.

At the foundation of managing clients' expectations is accepting the fact that nearly all projects should start with a large dose of investigative work. In other words, begin by troubleshooting because there always will be something wrong. You should consider this "discovery" process as a key service you provide on projects. No doubt it will require a pretty high percentage of your work time too.

It's in everyone's best interests to reveal what's wrong as early on as possible. By taking the initiative on this, you also establish your position as an advocate for transparency and as a professional. Will clients always appreciate this? No, but it's the right thing to do.

The bottom line is that clients want their expectations to be met. Your job is to make sure their expectations are as realistic as is possible and that you find a way to get the work done. Be careful not to set precedents that force you out of your strategy of working around 20 hours per week or reduce your pay rate.

Understand that expectations often come down to communication. Communicate effectively with clients about the good and the bad to shape their expectations in ways that benefit your working relationship.

I'd like to close this chapter with a couple of nice stories regarding client expectations. The first story is about a time when I thought I was doing poorly on a project. Everyone on the team just kept their heads down and slaved away. I felt sort of disconnected and received practically no feedback on my work. Toward the end of the project, I wasn't sure if they were thinking about letting me go. That was when the client totally surprised me by announcing that I was doing an amazing job. What? It's like that came out of nowhere.

I've learned that you just never know where you stand with people sometimes. This is especially the case when working remotely due to the limited interaction. Usually, clients only let you know about problems. But there have been other times when something has gone wrong but the client made a point of telling me that it wasn't my fault so I shouldn't worry about it. I appreciated the gesture.

The other story is about a rare time when I worked in-house at a new company. It was bordering on chaos most of the time. There was so much drama. No one had job descriptions. Everyone was trying to prove his or her value daily. The project was based around managing a type of data a certain way. I felt I had a decent handle on my part of the programming, but was as insecure as everyone else when it came to knowing if my performance was up to par.

Shortly after the project was finished, I walked into the office and people were looking at me. I didn't know what to think at that moment. Not that I'm a totally negative person but I couldn't help but think I was in big trouble or something went very wrong with the project. Then they all started clapping and recognized me for my key role in the success of the project.

So much for the accuracy of my expectations in these cases.

Chapter 10
Hiring Help

Unless you want to scale your business and manage a staff, I recommend only one reason to hire some daily help for your business: to have a marketing assistant. Why in the world would a programmer need a marketing assistant? It's simple, to let you focus more time on generating revenue as a programmer.

I'll get into my thoughts on hiring after I share a brief story about the first person I ever hired as a marketing assistant. As I started earning quite a bit of money, I decided that I didn't want to use my valuable programming time to research lead lists, send out résumés and such. So I decided to hire my first marketing assistant.

I posted an ad on Craigslist for someone who could conduct basic Web research, communicate decently in writing and verbally, and work part-time on contract in-house. Of course, I received a bunch of responses.

After a number of interviews, I had a meeting with a young woman who sounded promising. We rode the elevator up several floors and, honestly, she started to look very uncomfortable—as in ill. We reached the office but when we started talking, she seemed to look even worse. She explained that she was prone to motion sickness. The elevator ride was enough of a trigger, I guess. Let's just say that her emergency light suddenly turned on. I rushed her to the bathroom just in time.

Great first employee interview, huh. Well, I hired her. It didn't have anything to do with sympathy for her motion sickness issue at about the most awkward time it could happen. She was fully qualified and, most of all, very enthusiastic about the job and working with me. It turned out that she did great work as a marketing assistant. I advised her to take the stairs in the future.

Should you hire a marketing assistant? Maybe not right away when you launch your business. It might make more sense financially to wait until the money rolls in.

If and when you do hire someone, he or she will be tasked with screening contract lists on a daily or at least a weekly basis to identify appropriate contracts. As I've said, to keep your workload at the right level you must be on top of identifying attractive listings so you constantly have résumés flying out the door and interviews being scheduled. This takes time. And time is your limited resource to maintain your revenue stream. In other words, contracting this initial job-searching task ends up saving you money and minimizes part of the distraction of marketing.

All you have to do for this assistant is outline your detailed criteria about the type of contracts, submissions and starting dates you prefer, your wheelhouse set of skills, the length of the contracts, and other keywords that match your desired work. The contract pay rate isn't necessarily a deciding factor so I consider that when I review the opportunities individually. I actually developed a browser extension to automatically highlight keywords in job listings to make the process quite efficient.

Set up a simple process for your assistant to enter the URLs or other search results into a spreadsheet, checklist or other recordkeeping system that you prefer. This will serve as your action item list each week. Remember that contract listings really vary in how much detail they provide so the default is to apply for all relevant ones and then learn more about the work during the interview, if you get one.

Your assistant can work remotely if you really trust him or her to get tasks completed on time and in a reasonable amount of time. I tend to prefer that this person work in my office so I can provide supervision and be available to answer questions that come up.

Just so you know, I'd say that we identify 30 to 40 viable contracts per week. We submit my résumé online along with any other required information. If the agency representing the prospective client is interested in me, we set a date for an initial interview by phone or video call. I say that I average around three to four interviews each week. They usually last no more than one hour.

Serving as a programmer's marketing assistant is a great part-time job for a student or someone looking for some extra income. How much you pay your assistant will depend on the scope of work you establish and maybe the person's experience. If your pay is too low, you won't gain much loyalty and the quality of the person's work may not provide enough value. So be fair with pay to hire someone you can count on to help you make more money. It's a team effort.

Staffing agencies that establish you on their contractor call lists do a decent job of performing this screening process for you. Some are better than others. But you don't want to rely on them contacting you. It's far better to take the initiative to have your assistant scan online contract listings—most of which are posted by agencies—or do it yourself.

Scaling your business by hiring a staff of programmers lies outside the scope of what I'm proposing in this book. Managing others, even if they're all contractors, requires a lot of time and effort. It's a business model more along the lines of a staffing agency, only you'd be keeping the work in-house, so to speak.

I've had a bit of experience subcontracting and it didn't work well for me. There were some performance issues as well as communication challenges. Junior level programmers tend to avoid asking for help when they run into problems, so end up wasting a lot of time trying to figure out things themselves. It's easy to understand that they want to appear competent and able to work independently. Unfortunately, the result is lost time and revenue.

Even the basic economics of hiring programmers didn't make a lot of sense to me. I would secure the contract for my subcontractor and take my cut of the revenue. That subcontractor now would be paid less than actual market rates. Why wouldn't he or she just go after the contract directly to make more money? The only reason would be if it were my qualifications that earned the contracts because the subcontractor wasn't up to the necessary skill level.

But a junior level subcontractor introduces a whole other factor to the operational equation. You likely will need to spend at least a bit of time training the programmer. To minimize this, you'll only want to assign pieces of the projects that the person has the skills to handle right off. This means that the piece of the project should not involve problem-solving, just straightforward coding.

A key for junior developers is to keep their focus on getting the syntax correct, memorizing function names and basically the process of coding. Even for the coding that this person can manage independently, you'd likely need to provide ongoing supervision to ensure that the end product meets your standards.

How much of your contract rate do you pay a junior programmer? First off, the project must pay a high enough rate that you can afford to pay a subcontractor. Assuming that, about half the billing rate is standard.

One benefit for this junior programmer is that he or she probably wouldn't be qualified to get the contracts. So this is an opportunity for him or her to gain experience with a specific part of higher-profile project. It's also a chance for the programmer to pick up additional skills if some training is part of the arrangement. Don't necessarily shy away from offering some training, as that can build loyalty and benefits on projects down the road. You should expect to make approximately a two-month investment in guiding or training the programmer to align with your work process comfort zone.

An important consideration regarding hiring a marketing assistant or junior programmer is compatibility. This person must be able to communicate effectively with you. Also, his or her work style has to be a good fit or you'll end up being distracted. One trait I'd look for would be a professional attitude. The programming side is serious business, with deadlines and expectations for quality. My name is on the contract so this programmer must perform in a businesslike way.

I do want to mention that hiring a junior programmer means that this person would be a 1099 contractor for your company. Getting into the world of hiring W-2 employees opens a range of additional complications in running your business. That's when you must deal with different tax requirements, insurance coverage, maybe benefits, and even the need to provide equipment and other facilities. I have had no desire to build a company like this.

A marketing assistant also would be a 1099 contractor. It's clean and simple to manage.

Chapter 11
Self-Care

You need to be at your mental and physical best to cope with the long hours and stress of high-performance developer work like I'm proposing in this book. That means you've got to take care of yourself.

The following suggestions are based on my experience. If you have health conditions or concerns, you should see a healthcare professional.

Diet

I've found that I must make a special effort to keep hydrated while working. That doesn't mean drinking lots of coffee, tea, sports drinks or energy drinks. I simply drink water. If you're interested, you can find endless articles written by medical researchers about the health benefits of drinking water throughout the day. I'm a believer in proper hydration to maintain my health and stamina especially on intense workdays.

I've also got to say something about food. Justified or not, there's a stereotype of programmers at their workstations surrounded by empty chip bags, candy wrappers, soda cans, greasy pizza boxes and half-eaten cheeseburgers. This type of diet just isn't going to cut it for you to sustain your work performance. I like tasty snacks just as much as anyone, but it's nowhere near my core diet. And I take care to keep my salt intake low for the many health benefits.

Even if you don't have the time or desire to cook for yourself, you still can eat food that fuels your body and keeps your mind sharp. Whole foods, not processed ones, offer the most nutritional value in my opinion. Find take-out restaurants that offer healthful meals and keep things like fresh fruits, nuts and nutritious food bars around for quick snacks. Well-formulated food bars actually can be very good alternatives to the temptation of candy and other junk foods.

Sleep
I've got to get my sleep and so do you. Yes, there are times when my workload and deadlines require some late nights at the computer but that cannot be the general rule. If I don't get enough sleep, I'll lose my focus and the quality of my work will suffer. I just can't afford that. If I get drowsy during the day, maybe I'll take a short nap. But it's a good idea to set an alarm to prevent crashing for hours or an afternoon.

Certainly, programming can be very intense work. You get on a roll coding a module and you can lose track of time, whether or not you've eaten, and about everything else. It's easy to get totally immersed in work when you're in the middle of searching for the root cause of a bug and become hyper-focused on finding that piece of pesky code that's screwing up a function. These situations can get you very stimulated as well as stressed, in a positive way. So it can be rough going to sleep when your brain is still racing.

I think it's good to find ways to detach from work and calm down before hitting the sheets. I'm not a TV watcher but that can work for some people. Music can be a great solution as long as it doesn't make you revved up even more. Some folks read a novel or anything other than work related material. I really enjoy audio books. Meditation or yoga can be fantastic to calm your mind and body too. Figure out what works for you to prevent restless nights that come back to haunt you during the workday.

Exercise

Here's another stereotype out there about developers: they have little interest in exercise. All I can say is that I need to have an effective outlet to combat stress and help me get sound sleep at night. Exercise works. I took up jiu jitsu, the Brazilian martial art, as my main way to get vigorous exercise. It's a fantastic workout, keeping me limber and in decent shape. There's the extra social benefit of working out with great people who rarely have anything to do with programming.

I'm certainly not a fitness expert, but I know that just about everyone can find some type of exercise to improve or maintain his or her health. Lots of programmers go for walks, long runs or bike rides every day. Find a form of exercise or sport that you enjoy and add it to your daily business calendar like any important commitment. Investing in your health pays off in your bank account.

Unplugging with others

If you only hang around IT people and other developers, your conversations are going to turn to work related topics. It's a good idea to unplug from the industry on a regular basis to clear your head. Jiu jitsu is one of those things that I do to unplug with others. I also go outside during good weather to walk in the neighborhood or a park to be around people.

It's not difficult to find a diverse crowd through non-work related classes, family members, activities, friends and personal interests. Dating is a favorite diversion for many of us who are single. Even though relationships can be very challenging when your work-life balance is heavily weighted on the work side, that doesn't mean you should resign yourself to being a total recluse. We all need friends and the potential for more to keep a healthy perspective on life.

Attitude

I reward myself for big and small accomplishments. Maybe it's my bias, but I think the best rewards are ones that are personally meaningful rather than what others say are signs of success.

This doesn't necessarily have anything to do with spending lots of money on stuff you may or may not need. It could range from going to a film with a friend or adopting a dog. As a stress killer and way to relax, I've found that there's nothing better than a good massage.

Sure you might have had your eye on a nicer apartment, new car, mountain bike, big screen TV, VR gear or drone. Maybe I'm practical, but I think that a nice reward is to hire a maid to keep my home clean and tidy. This also saves me time on chores that aren't so fun. The key is to experience the fruits of your labor often enough so it feels worthwhile besides just saving money for the future.

A philosophical point I feel compelled to mention is the value I find in understanding what it means to live in the present moment. Part of this is about rewarding yourself now rather than always later. The main aspect is being engaged with or truly experiencing your life while you're living it. Be there for yourself and for others when you're with them.

The popular buzzword associated with this is mindfulness. When you get it about being present, you probably will be less stressed from work and maintain a better outlook on life in general. This is true at least for me. There are some great books on this subject, so check them out if you're interested.

Personal hygiene
I prefer not to get into this at any length, maybe because it falls into the less savory category of stereotypes. Let's just say that part of being a business professional involves personal hygiene (showers are a good thing), grooming (maybe the occasional stylish haircut) and wearing clean clothes (enough said).

Yes, regular dental, vision and physical checkups prevent bigger problems down the road. Even if you don't have much personal or visual contact with clients, take care of these things to feel good about yourself.

The sad consequences of the dark side
Unfortunately, I've seen what happens to developers who don't take care of themselves. They can be terribly affected by chronic illnesses, emotional breakdowns and serious personal hygiene issues that result in lost contracts and destroyed personal relationships.

Yes, this can happen with anyone whose work-life balance becomes out of whack. But a pretty high percentage of developers tend to be less socially well adjusted and not ones to address health issues until they become quite severe. I don't have statistics on this, just my years of experience in the industry and what I've observed.

So I urge you to eat right, get your sleep, exercise daily and learn to unplug completely from work regularly. You'll do better work, project professionalism to your clients and just plan feel better.

Chapter 12
Final Thoughts

If you have reasonable programming skills, can communicate fairly well with clients and understand how to operate a simple business, you can earn $450,000 a year working remotely. I'm proof that the strategy I've outlined in this book actually works. And you don't have to live in Silicon Valley to do it.

What are the key points to remember from my experience? Position yourself with sound skills using the right tools, gain some experience to build your résumé, grow your ability to adapt to tools and the market, learn how to operate a business properly and know what the market wants—always playing to the hot market areas. About the market, it's easy to respond to contracting opportunities because prospective clients usually tell us exactly what they want in every contract description and, most of the time, how much they pay.

Nothing would thrill me more than to hear that you're on your way to earning the big bucks. It would be an honor to know this book has helped you. Please feel free to forward your stories about working as a remote developer.

Remotely Rich